THE RELIGIOUS SOC... of FRIENDS "might be thought of as a prism through which the DIVINE LIGHT passes to become visible in a spectrum of many colours; many more in their richness than words alone can express." Faith + Practice.

The title panel, The prism

Since the dawn of recorded history, craftspeople have used their skills to tell stories. Such a record is the Quaker Tapestry – made in a form known as 'narrative crewel embroidery'. As with the famous Bayeux Tapestry, it is a hanging which tells a story. The Quaker Tapestry has been described as a celebration of Quaker experience and insights over 350 years, though Quakers would hasten to add that they do not, by any means, lay sole claim to them. Nevertheless, it is a timely reminder of the contribution these non-conformists have made to the modern world.

How it all began

Clockwise frmo top left:
Anne Wynn-Wilson in the 1980s
One of Anne's samplers of the Bayeux Tapestry
Jonathan Stocks in the early 1980s
Jonathan at Kendal in 2001

It all began in a Quaker Sunday school in the south of England in 1981...

The original intention was for the children to make a long scroll depicting some of the stories of the first Quakers in the mid 17th century. One of the children, then aged 11, thought this was going to be yet another Sunday morning colouring in and asked, "Can't we do something more exciting? Like mosaic or collage?". His teacher to whom the remark was made was Anne Wynn-Wilson, an experienced embroiderer. Jonathan threw the first pebble in the pond, that January morning in 1981, and the ripples still continue today...

At the time Anne Wynn-Wilson was completing her City and Guilds embroidery thesis on the 11th century crewel embroidery, the Bayeux Tapestry. Anne devised an embroidery scheme that would incorporate some of the design elements of the Bayeux within the Quaker Tapestry. It would be unified in its design, fabric and materials, yet diverse enough in technique and subject matter to draw together groups of people with differing interests and abilities. It was decided at this point to develop separate panels, each illustrating an aspect of Quaker history or work. The number eventually expanded to 77 panels.

Designers came forward, embroidery groups were formed and training workshops were arranged. Altogether more than 4,000 men, women and children in 15 countries have 'had a hand' in the creation of the Quaker Tapestry, which was eventually finished in 1996.

At the heart of the tapestry scheme were the embroidery workshops. It was here that beginners learned the stitches and met people from other groups. Research and design ideas could be discussed and work in progress could be assessed. Many of the 4,000 people involved in making the Tapestry were completely without experience of embroidery.

Detail from panel D1
George Fox: Lichfield, Pendle Hill

Below left: For the central figure of George Fox, dressed in his leather breeches, Anne did lots of research. She asked her husband, David, to pose in his walking trousers.

Below right: Whenever possible, photographs were used in the design. St Andrew's Church at Sedbergh gave the embroiderers ideas for the colours and texture of the stone.

When the war b
we dec

For some Quakers, working on a panel had deep meaning. A retired engineer who embroidered a Nantucket whaling ship on panel F12 later wrote:

"That week's work is likely to be more enduring than anything else I have ever done in my life, which is really quite surprising. In working life I built factories all over the world that cost millions of pounds and the Tapestry is a tiny little thing but it is obviously going to endure in time more than any of these other things. Already I know some of the factories I built have been closed and demolished."

Stories behind the stitches

Elizabeth Fry

> ## "*Punishment is not for revenge, but to lessen crime and reform the criminal*"

Elizabeth Fry (1780-1845)

In the early 18th century women were transported to the Australian penal colonies for crimes such as pickpocketing or prostitution.

On arrival, they would serve in factories or in private homes for up to seven years. Elizabeth Fry, the Quaker prison reformer, arranged for each female transportee to be given materials with which to make a patchwork quilt during the hazardous voyage. She hoped this would lead to their rehabilitation and employment.

Panel E6 in progress

The Quaker Tapestry woollen cloth

The original woollen cloth showing the nine colours of wool

In the 1980s original woollen cloth was woven especially for the Tapestry in Somerset by the weavers Talbot Potter and John Lennon. The colour was based on the local stone, known as 'Quantock' sandstone. Nine different shades of wool were identified and selected to be woven using a random warp, which produced a low-key stripe. The stripe and the weave provide a guide to keep the line of the lettering and buildings vertical.

The cloth used now in the embroidery workshops and kits is woven in southwest Wales by a company called 'Melin Teifi', which is on the same site as the Welsh Woollen Museum, 15 miles inland from Cardigan Bay. A plain weave woollen cloth with 16 ends and 18-19 picks to the inch is woven by Eric Faulkner and warped by Brian Cook. There are 7 colours of sheep's wool in the warp and 2 in the weft, using 7 different breeds of British sheep including Shetland and Jacob. No dyes are used. The cloth is washed and scoured with soda and soap, and dried and pressed at the museum in Wales. It is not treated or moth-proofed in any way.

The Welsh Woollen Museum site is open to the public 7 days a week from April to September 10am-5pm and 5 days (Tuesday-Saturday) between October and March.

Top right: Quantock sandstone
Below: Raymond Jones, designer
of the new woollen cloth
Bottom right: John Lennon and
Talbot Potter, weavers of the original cloth.

The Quaker stitch

The Quaker stitch

Anne Wynn-Wilson designed the stitch used to create the letters for the Quaker Tapestry - she didn't know at the time that she was creating a new stitch. Combining two of the oldest stitches - the 'stem' and the 'split'- makes the Quaker stitch. When Anne was compiling a stitch manual for workshops she asked experts at the Royal School of Needlework to identify the stitch for her. They too were baffled at the new technique and soon realised that she had created a new stitch. They asked Anne if she would like to call it the 'Quaker stitch' after the project for which it had been designed.

The embroidery workshops

The embroidery workshops continue today at Kendal, and elsewhere when requested by groups, to share the stitches and techniques of this unique style of community textile. The workshops cater for both the absolute beginner and the experienced embroiderer, whether producing simple embroidery from a Quaker Tapestry kit or embarking on a large community project.

Why is it called a 'Tapestry' when it is embroidery?

The 'crewel embroidery' technique, just like the Bayeux Tapestry, is designed to dance freely across the surface of the fabric, quite distinct from canvas work stitches, which are regulated by the grid of the canvas. Canvas work is frequently known by the misnomer 'tapestry work'. In a true tapestry the design is woven directly into the warp threads, using the special technique of tapestry weaving. All three methods have been used over the years to make hangings which tell a story. The French word for a worker in these techniques is *tapissière*. No wonder there is confusion in naming these textiles!

Below: Bridget Guest overseeing students at an embroidery workshop in Kendal

Lettering showing the Quaker stitch

Opposite: detail from panel D12 Ecology

Stories behind the stitches

The slave trade

By the middle of the 18th century there was a rise of anti-slavery feeling among Quakers on both sides of the Atlantic. But the slow process of persuasion among Friends was slow, and it was not until 1776 that Quakers finally ceased owning slaves.

From 1772 Quakers were instrumental in protesting to Parliament about the terrible conditions suffered by slaves who were transported to British colonies, and this unrest had implications in the Americas.

In 1807, through the efforts of William Wilberforce and spurred along by the hard work of British Quakers, the slave trade in Britain was abolished and England became a home for many escaped American slaves. By 1833 the British Parliament had passed the Emancipation Act, slavery became illegal throughout the British Colonies and Canada had become an even safer haven. In Canada the Society of Friends purchased eight hundred acres of land for escaped slaves.

By 1850 an extensive network of escape routes had developed from the Southern plantations into Canada. These became known as the Underground Railroad, so called because the people involved spoke in railway terms to prevent anyone knowing the actual routes or details of those who assisted them.

There are many stories of narrow escapes: the children's work at the bottom of panel F10 The Underground Railroad shows some of the runaway slaves hiding in a grain cart with a false bottom, pursued by bounty hunters with their dogs.

Many safe houses had secret rooms, cellars or lofts, cleverly concealed from view. The secrecy protected both escapees and helpers – as the sheriffs were not above intimidation to extract information, the less known the better. To protect people, no records were written down, so estimates of those who gained freedom travelling the Underground Railroad vary from 40,000 to 100,000.

Part-completed panel, F3 The slave trade, embroidered in Kendal in 1995

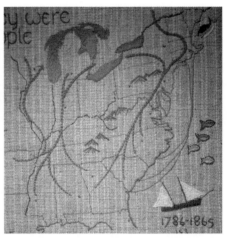

Detail from panel F10 The Underground Railroad

Along the route slaves took refuge in barns, swamps, woods, ditches and caves. They travelled mainly at night using the star patterns and secret codes held in the words of gospel songs such as 'Steal Away to Jesus'; 'Swing Low Sweet Chariot' and 'The Drinking Gourd'. The codes told them in which direction to travel.

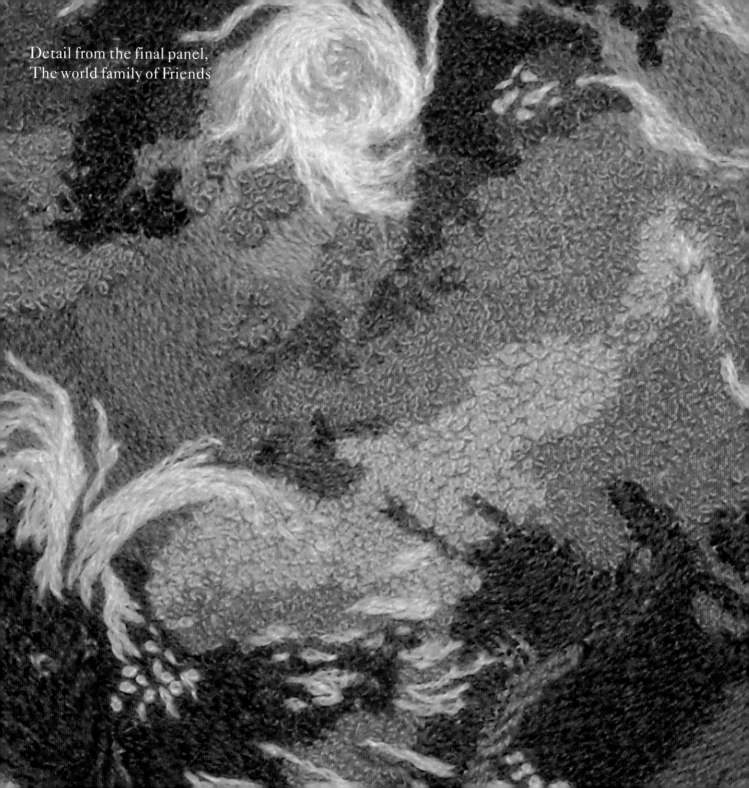

Detail from the final panel,
The world family of Friends

The 15 countries involved in making the Quaker Tapestry:

Australia & Tasmania
Britain
Canada
Chile
Eire
France
East Germany
Japan
Mexico
The Netherlands
New Zealand
South Africa
Switzerland
United States of America

Barrett Friendship Quilt

*'o magic sleep,
o comfortable bird,
that broodest o'er
the troubled sea of
the mind til it is
hushed and smooth'*

Quotation by John Keats
embroidered on the
Barrett Friendship Quilt

Subsidiary display: Weapons of the Spirit

One of the other displays at the permanent home of the Quaker Tapestry in Kendal features the fascinating 'Barrett Friendship Quilt'.

This embroidered counterpane represents a record of two families brought together by a marriage – a record that includes the husband and wife's close friends and relations, many of whom were involved in the various art movements and the industrial progress of the 19th century.

The creation of such 'friendship' counterpanes and quilts was a well-established tradition by the late 1800s. Their purposes varied. They might be sewn to raise money for the restoration of a church or as a way of declaring a shared belief – such as those quilts made by individuals within the anti-slavery movement. In the harsh conditions for early settlers in America the making of friendship quilts, like diaries, provided a means of chronicling the struggles and hopes of families. The communal creation of these quilts in 'quilting bees' was also a way of bringing communities together.

Quilts of course, unlike diaries, were practical things – warm reminders of friends, family and journeys covered as individuals trekked from east to west coast in search of a better life.

Although, appropriately enough for a bed covering, this friendship counterpane is decorated with many images and words associated with sleep, night and dreams, the stitches are also permeated with a theme of the passing of time.

Subsidiary displays at Kendal

Some areas of the exhibition at Kendal are designed to house changing displays including costume and other Quaker artefacts. We have featured such themes as 'science', 'marriage', 'schools', 'Quaker Tapestry inspired textiles' and 'new' panels, 'botanists and plant hunters', 'abolition of the slave trade' and 'Quaker responses to conflict over 350 years'. Future displays may include topics such as 'early railways' and 'industrial welfare'.

Left and above: Details from the
Barrett Friendship Quilt

Stories behind the stitches

Early railways

This panel bears witness to the friendship between Edward Pease, a wealthy coal-owning Quaker, and the engineer, George Stephenson. Together, with the backing of Quaker bankers, they created the world's first public steam-operated railway from Stockton to Darlington in 1825.

At the bottom of the panel, beneath arches, are embroidered scenes that connect Quakers to the railway enterprise.

At the far right, a printing press indicates the work of George Bradshaw who introduced printed railway timetables.

Next to this, Thomas Edmondson, inventor of the pasteboard railway ticket, is commemorated with the scene of a Victorian family paying their fares.

Under the central arch is the first passenger coach, built by Thomas Worsdell and painted yellow at George Stephenson's request. Navvies, laying lines, represent the firm of Robert Ransome and Charles May, which had devised a system for securing sleepers to the rails.

Lastly, a foundry is shown with its incandescent molten metal. The image is suggestive of Coalbrookdale where John Wilkinson produced cast-iron for the tracks.

*"We have spent hours here, almost tearfully inspired.
Like the Bayeux it will be here in a 1000 years time.
This has been the delight of our holiday."*

Rev'd & Mrs R Chudley, Cornwall - October 2007

*"We have so enjoyed seeing this wonderful exhibition.
It is amazing, inspiring and so relevant to today's world.
Loved the extra exhibition of Annette Mortlock too.
Thank You"*

Margaret & Harold Neale, Norfolk - August 2007

"I could have stayed all day"

Martha Johnson, New Hampshire USA - May 2008

*"Very interesting and very beautiful exibition. The tearoom
is also nice and the staff are very sympathic and nice! This house
is like an island of peace in the heart of the town. Thank you."*

Claire D'Albignac, Voiron, France - July 2006

Stories behind the stitches

Quaker botanists

Across the centre of the Botanists panel pink, yellow, red and white flowering plants are seen as if through a trellis. To the left of each one, is stitched its Latin name. Some of the featured trees, shrubs or blooms, such as *Chelone obliqua* and magnolia, may be found in the gardens of Kendal Meeting House.

Most of the plants were found by Quaker plant-hunters and classified by Quaker collectors. Eleven of these men are listed in two embroidered rows, one above and one below the central plant design.

In the bottom row are two Quakers whose friendly correspondence lasted for many years without them ever meeting. John Bartram, born in 1699, was a Pennsylvanian farmer who supplied collectors with plants. Peter Collinson was a merchant whose shipping contacts gave him access to the plant hunters of North America. He asked John Bartram to supply him with a curious plant that the Native Americans called Tipitiwitchet. Eight years later the specimen arrived, just a few months before Peter Collinson's death. Today this plant is known as the Venus Fly-trap.

Sidney Parkinson, whose name can be found in the top row, was neither plant-hunter nor collector. He was an artist on James Cook's first voyage to the South Seas, employed to illustrate the botanical finds. Despite the ravages of flies on paper and paints, Sidney Parkinson left many sketches and watercolours of the voyage before his death from disease, in 1771, on the homeward journey. He was not yet thirty years old.

Chelone obliqua

Detail from the Botanists panel

Is the Quaker Tapestry finished or will more panels be produced?

In 1996 when the 77th panel was completed, the committee decided to stop producing further panels. The Somerset weavers had retired and the original woollen cloth had all been used. 77 panels of embroidery was a huge number to display in one exhibition and when the permanent home at Kendal had been established in 1994 the committee decided that their role was complete. However, Quakerism still continues today and there are many more stories to tell, both from history and from subjects concerning Quakers today...

So panels do continue to be made by other groups who are inspired to take up the needle and the challenge of embarking on a panel of embroidery. In 2007 Quakers in Australia invited Bridget Guest, who teaches the embroidery today, to visit New South Wales to teach two workshops in Sydney and the Blue Mountains. Students attended from different parts of Australia and Tasmania to learn the skills and to pass them on to others joining the Australian project. News and progress of these, and further groups inspired by the tapestry can be found within the Quaker Tapestry Newsletters and on the website.

Left: Students at an embroidery workshop in Kendal
Far left: Rachel Abbott sewing panel F3 The slave trade
Opposite: Maurice Hopper embroidering his own panel design 'Working in the Silence'

Stories behind the stitches

The Netherlands

Laura van Honk's house in Amsterdam was a few hundred metres from Anne Frank's home and is shown in the panel on the right. She and other Young Friends smuggled valuables belonging to Jews out of the country and then helped with their emigration. Laura later received Israel's Yad Vashem medal for helping Jews during the war.

We have developed an interactive CD-Rom based on extensive research in both Holland and Israel, which lets you explore the stories of bravery and tragedy, despair and hope through word, image and sound. The CD-Rom "These Houses Hold Secrets" can be viewed within the exhibition at Kendal, and through it you can discover the efforts made by Dutch Quakers during the 2nd World War to save the lives of Jewish children and families.

Laura van Honk's house in Amsterdam

Detail of panel F22 The Netherlands 1940-1945

Panel references

Each of the 77 panels has a reference code; this was
originally used during the early 1980s to separate
the subject matter into categories or group headings.
These were contained within the 1959 edition
of the book Quaker Faith and Practice. This was fully
revised in 1995 and is usually rewritten two or
three times a century.

The letters and numbers are of no particular
importance to the viewer, merely a reference guide
for identification purposes. Generally the panels
are displayed at the exhibitions in historical date
order from the 1650s onwards.

Further information on the panels
shown with * after the reference code is
included on the hand-held audio guides
available for use at the exhibition.

No.*	Title				
	The Prism	D1	George Fox: Lichfield, Pendle Hill	F5	Delegation to the Czar 1854
A1 *	George Fox's convincement	D2	Simplicity	F6	Relief work: British Isles
A2	James Nayler	D3	Persecution in Oxford	F7	Relief work overseas
A3	James Parnell; Meeting for Sufferings	D4*	Coalbrookdale	F8	Friends Ambulance Unit
A4	Richard Sellar	D5	Innocent trades	F9	Northern Ireland: Reconciliation
A5*	Voyage of the Woodhouse	D6*	Merchants	F10	The Underground Railroad
A6	John Woolman	D7*	Railways	F11	Penn and Pennsylvania
A7	Conscientious objection	D8*	Botanists	F12*	Nantucket and Milford Haven
A8	Manchester Conference 1895	D9*	True health	F13	Dolgellau and Pennsylvania
A9	Oaths	D10*	Scientists	F14	New Zealand/Aotearoa
B1*	Firbank Fell: George Fox preaching	D11	Industrial welfare	F15	Workcamps
B2	Mary Fisher	D12*	Ecology	F16*	Peace embassies
B3	John Bright	D13	Scott-Bader Commonwealth	F17	Vigils for peace
B4	Publishers of Truth	E1	George Fox at Ulverston: healing	F18	World Conference 1991
B5	Stephen Grellet	E2	John Bellers	F19	South Africa
B6	Woodbrooke	E3*	Bankering	F20	Tasmania
B7	Service overseas	E4	Criminal justice	F21	Canada
B8	Quaker Peace Action Caravan	E5	Elizabeth Fry	F22	The Netherlands 1940-1945
C1*	Swarthmoor Hall	E6*	Elizabeth Fry and the patchwork quilts	Final*	The world family of Friends
C2	Margaret Fell	E7	Adult schools		
C3	Keeping the meeting	E8	Ireland: The great hunger 1845-8		
C4*	Meeting houses	E9*	Mary Hughes		
C5	Meeting houses overseas	E10*	Unemployment		
C6	Meeting houses in the community	E11	Friends Provident Institution		
C7*	Schools	E12	William Allen		
C8*	Marriage	F1	George Fox in Derby gaol		
C9	Pilgrimages	F2	The Penn and Meade trial		
C10	Children and young people	F3	The slave trade		
C11	Leaveners	F4	Daniel Wheeler		

Stories behind the stitches

Scientists

All from humble backgrounds, the three Quaker scientists in this panel became internationally recognised: John Dalton founded modern chemistry and devised an atomic theory which enabled him to determine the atomic weight of certain gases; Arthur Eddington was one of the foremost British astrophysicists of the 20th century and Kathleen Lonsdale, whose work was crucial in the development of crystallography, was an active peace worker and an advocate of penal reform.

A fellow scientist wrote of Kathleen Lonsdale: "She loved crystallography, and she loved pictures that were beautiful." It seems appropriate that a crystal structure, with which she was associated, has been threaded into the artwork of the panel.

When he was twenty-six, John Dalton bought what he thought were sober blue stockings for his mother's birthday and was astonished to be told that they were red. In this way he identified his colour-blindness that later became known as Daltonism. He developed an atomic theory and invented chemical symbols that he arranged into a table. Part of this table can be seen above his portrait on the panel. One of the symbols shown represents Azote, which was the old term for nitrogen.

For a decade, it was said, only Arthur Eddington, other than Einstein, understood the theory of relativity. One of the things the theory suggested was that light would bend under the influence of gravity when close to a star. To confirm this, Eddington travelled to the island of Principe to photograph an eclipse. The dark imposing silhouette of the island can be seen on the panel. Although the day was cloudy the results of Eddington's efforts demonstrated that Einstein was correct. These scientists were three of the eighty or so Quakers who have been Fellows of the Royal Society.

Detail of Sir Arthur Stanley Eddington from panel D10 Scientists

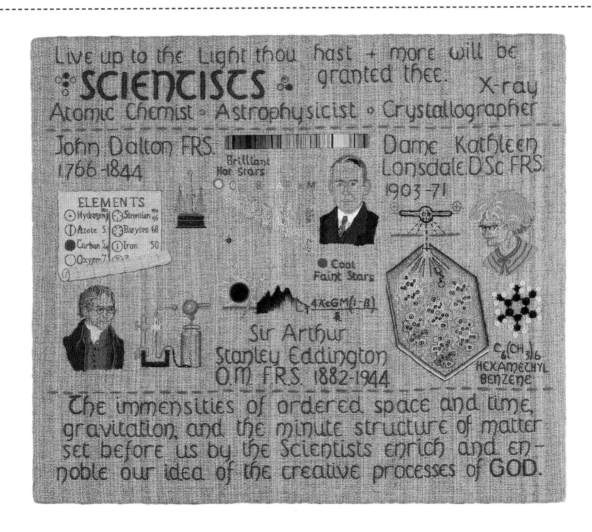

Why the Quaker Tapestry came to Kendal

Anne Wynn-Wilson and those who took part in the scheme were always seeking a permanent home for the tapestry. A meeting between Anne and a Kendal Friend in 1991 led to the creation of a permanent exhibition centre in the heart of what is known to Quakers as '1652 Country', the area in which Quakerism was born. Kendal Meeting House, a beautiful Grade II listed building in the Lake District, was at the time far too big for the local Quakers. A joint agreement allowed the building to be shared by the Quaker Tapestry and Kendal Friends.

Between the first major public exhibition in 1989 at Aberdeen Art Gallery and the opening of the permanent exhibition at Kendal in April 1994, the embroideries travelled all over Britain and Ireland, to Bayeux in France and to five states in North America.

The Quaker Tapestry:
travelling 'Roadshow exhibition'

Each winter, when the Exhibition Centre in Kendal is closed, 39 of the 77 panels of embroidery go on tour for a month to give more people the opportunity to see the tapestry. Since its first public exhibition, the Quaker Tapestry has been displayed in over 160 venues in the UK, Europe and America. The annual Tapestry Roadshow is an unqualified success, attracting thousands of visitors to each venue.

Education

As a charitable company, the Quaker Tapestry provides informal learning opportunities for those of all ages. It does this through the exhibition itself and through interpretative material, including hand held multi-lingual audio guides, films, books and pamphlets. Subsidiary exhibitions add to these educational opportunities. More formal learning opportunities are available to schools, colleges and study groups through educational visits and activities at the Quaker Tapestry. All profits generated through admission fees, tearoom and sales of goods and services are reinvested back into the Quaker Tapestry.

The Tapestry Tearoom
at the exhibition in Kendal

The tearoom was opened in March 2002 with the intention of providing good, wholesome, tasty and healthy food for visitors to the tapestry. Local produce is used whenever possible to provide an eclectic mix of vegetarian food to suit all tastes. In fact, most of our customers do not realise that it is exclusively vegetarian fare – they just come in to sample the good food and friendly atmosphere always at hand. The tearoom quickly gained a good reputation with the local people of Kendal who use the facilities all year round. We cater for those with special dietary needs such as vegans, and those with allergies. The locally-sourced produce is baked on the premises. In November 2007 the tearoom gained the national award from the Vegetarian Society for 'Best Provision for Vegetarians at a Visitor Attraction'.

The award-winning exhibition centre at Kendal

The Quaker Tapestry Exhibition was awarded 'Small Visitor Attraction of the Year 2008' by the Cumbria and Northwest Tourism boards.

Gift shop

The gift shop in Kendal and at the roadshows carries a wide range of tasteful products linked to the tapestry. Images from the panels are captured on postcards, greetings cards, bookmarks, embroidery kits, calendars, toys, books and many other items suitable for adults and children alike.